Adventures in Canadian History

THE MEN IN SHEEPSKIN COATS

PIERRE BERTON

THE MEN IN SHEEPSKIN COATS

ILLUSTRATIONS BY PAUL MCCUSKER

M&S

An M&S Paperback Original from
McClelland & Stewart Inc.
The Canadian Publishers

An M&S Paperback Original from McClelland & Stewart Inc.

First printing March 1992

Canadian Cataloguing in Publication Data

Berton, Pierre, 1920-
The men in sheepskin coats

(Adventures in Canadian history. Canada moves west)
"An M&S paperback original."
Includes index.
ISBN 0-7710-1438-4

1. Ukrainians – Canada, Western – History – Juvenile literature. 2. Canada, Western – Emigration and immigration – History – Juvenile literature.
3. Ukraine – Emigration and immigration – History – Juvenile literature.
4. Immigrants – Canada, Western – History – Juvenile literature. 5. Aliens – Canada, Western – History – Juvenile literature. I. Title. II. Series: Berton, Pierre, 1920- . Adventures in Canadian history. Canada moves west.

FC3230.U5B4 1992   j971.2'00491791   C92-093665-2
F1060.97.U5B4 1992

Series design by Tania Craan
Original text design by Martin Gould
Cover illustration by Scott Cameron
Interior illustrations by Paul McCusker
Maps by James Loates
Editor: Peter Carver

Typesetting by M&S
Printed and bound in Canada

McClelland & Stewart Inc.
The Canadian Publishers
481 University Avenue
Toronto, Ontario
M5G 2E9

Contents

Map appears on page 10

Everyone who lives in this country is an immigrant – or a descendant of immigrants. This includes the aboriginal peoples, those native Canadians whose ancestors crossed the land bridge between Siberia and Alaska thousands of years ago. For there was a time when Asia, Africa, and Europe were populated, but no human beings roamed this continent.

Few immigrants to Canada have had an easy time. Neither the land nor the people has welcomed newcomers. The land may seem beautiful to us, but it was harsh and forbidding to those who had to contend with a savage terrain just emerging from the Ice Age. The French and English who invaded the new country after the fifteenth century had to contend, in their turn, with those who had come before. So it was then; so it is today.

We do not welcome strangers to Canada, whether they be Asians, Ukrainians, or even English. There was a time in this country when signs were posted in store windows announcing: "NO ENGLISH NEED APPLY." In our own time

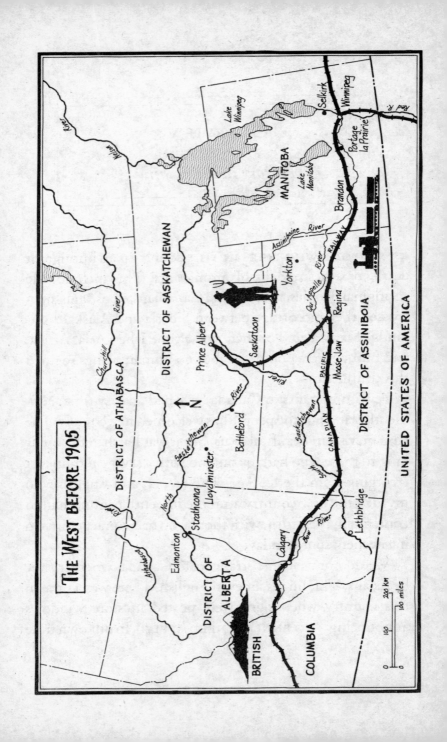

The West before 1905

we have seen this kind of unthinking attitude applied to Sikhs, Pakistanis, Chinese, Japanese, and Italians. Every one of us, then, springs from a strange culture much misunderstood by those who came before. Every one of us is the descendant of immigrants who were themselves looked on with suspicion and even hatred. That process continues to this day, as wave after wave of new strangers reach our shores.

Why, one wonders, do they come at all? The answer, in most cases, is that they have had to. The people you will meet in this book had little choice, if they were to free themselves of the poverty and hopelessness of their own land. And that still applies today. We are, in many respects, a nation of refugees – from war, from dictatorship, from overcrowding, from want.

But there is another side to the coin. Those who made the difficult choice to leave hearth and home to seek a new life in a new world were also the most daring members of their communities. It requires an enormous act of courage and will to say goodbye forever to friends and family, as the immigrants from Eastern Europe did at the turn of the century. They were, as this book makes clear, a steadfast, enterprising, and hardy group of people; most immigrants are. The very nature of their decision makes them so.

They were never a liability, as many suggested at the time. They were an asset, as we now know, for they brought something of their own culture with them and thus enriched the culture of the new land they themselves helped to build. The story has no ending, for they are still arriving on our shores, these strange new people, helping to enrich us all, as the men and women in sheepskin coats did a century ago.

CHAPTER ONE
Josef Oleskow's dream

THIS IS THE STORY of one of the greatest mass movements in history – the filling up of an empty land, a thousand miles (1,600 km) broad, with more than one million people in less than one generation. It is the story of the opening of the Canadian West, from Winnipeg to the Rocky Mountains, in the years between 1896 and 1914. It is the story of the creation of a state within a state, and the transformation of a nation.

It begins, of course, with the Canadian Pacific Railway – but that is another tale. British Columbia was promised a national railway in return for joining Confederation. The famous line was completed in 1885 as a result of that promise. But depression struck, and in spite of the fact that the railway was supposed to bring people out to the empty Northwest, scarcely anybody came. For ten years, the land remained almost as empty as it had been in the days when the Hudson's Bay Company was in control.

But there was treasure in the West – not gold but rich, black soil, scoured off the old rocks of the Canadian Shield by the moving glaciers of the last ice age, and pushed by a bulldozer action onto the land we call the prairies. This vast acreage of topsoil, perfect for grain growers, would help make Canada the breadbasket of the world.

But this was also dry country. Little rain fell. The winters were cold. The kind of wheat that had been grown in the southern parts of the world would not flourish in Canada. Furthermore, men were needed – and women too – to harvest the grain. In the Russian Ukraine, there were men and women aplenty, most of them hungry and badly nourished, some of whom had their eyes on the plains of Canada, and many who dreamed of a better world across the sea.

So let us meet one of these dreamers. His name was Josef Oleskow, a Slavic professor of agriculture from Eastern Europe, and in the hot summer of 1895 he made his way by train on a journey of discovery to the Canadian West.

Anyone who saw him would know he was a stranger to the country. His hair, dark and thick, was not parted, but combed straight back, European style. His moustache didn't droop over his lips in the North American way, but turned sharply upward, into two fierce points. He was dressed formally and neatly – dark suit, high starched collar, thick tie.

He was a handsome man of thirty-five years, with dark, intelligent eyes and regular features, and he was enchanted by the New World. The people, he thought, were so clean and, equally important, so independent. Here, there were no lords, no peasants. Here, everyone was a master!

And officials did not act as they did back home. They

were workers just like everybody else. They had no special privileges. Their offices were operated like stores. Why, you could walk in without even bowing! And the man behind the desk – even a cabinet minister – would probably keep his hat on.

But the *waste!* For two days, Dr. Oleskow's train plunged through the blackened forests of the Canadian Shield. These vast stretches of burned timber were a painful sight to him – a cemetery of dead trees. Apparently nobody had bothered to put out the flames that were ruining the land. Back in his native Ruthenia, then a part of the Ukraine in the Carpathian Mountains, wood was the most precious of all commodities. People hoarded it. But here the professor saw Canadians destroying their heritage. Why, he discovered, when they cleared the land they actually tossed the stumps into the nearest ravine!

The train left the blackened desert of the Shield and burst into the prairies. Here were other wonders. The Canadians, the professor realized, had an axe with a curved handle that fitted the shape of the hand. It was strange to him. He tested it and wondered why his own countrymen had failed to improve the design of their own farm implements, in spite of several centuries of toil.

Then as the train passed through the grainfields of Manitoba, he saw that nobody was using a sickle or a scythe. Machines, not men, were harvesting the wheat. If a man didn't own a machine he could always rent one from a neighbour.

At Portage la Prairie he watched these marvellous

machines follow one another in a staggered row across the wide fields, and marvelled at the horses that drew them. These were not the skinny, miserable nags of his native Carpathian mountains, but big, husky animals with real leather harnesses.

And yet the land was so empty! The only city of any consequence was Winnipeg. From Portage the plains rolled westward without a fence, the soil undisturbed by a plough. The waist-high buffalo grass was broken only by a thin network of trails that were really nothing but ruts. The occasional river valley was bordered by cottonwood and wolf willow. Indians in brightly-coloured blankets squatted in groups on the station platforms. Mountains of buffalo bones lined the track in the far west.

But where were the farms? Strung out along the railway the professor found a series of tiny settlements – mere clusters of frame buildings lining wooden sidewalks. Regina, the capital of what was then called the North West Territories, the so-called Queen City of the Plains, had fewer than two thousand people, huddled in wooden shacks that straggled for two miles (3.2 km) across a plain that was as flat as a kitchen table.

Saskatoon scarcely existed – just a railway station and a few houses. Calgary was a glorified cowtown of four thousand. Edmonton was little more than a trading post. These were primitive settlements. Calgary's dusty streets stank of horse manure. And Regina stank too from the hotel slops that drenched the main street. In Edmonton you could hear the piercing squeal of the ungreased Red River carts drawn along Portage Avenue by oxen and ponies. In the smaller villages, cows, pigs, and chickens wandered loose.

These little islands of civilization were lost in the great sweep of the prairies – wave after wave of grassland, rolling west towards the foothills, so that the country, from the Red River to the Rockies, looked like a prehistoric ocean that had somehow been frozen. But, as Dr. Oleskow noted, the earth everywhere was rich and black. His own countrymen were starved for land. He realized that this empty country could be their salvation.

He went as far west as Edmonton. A handful of his fellow countrymen had preceded him and he was astonished by their new prosperity. Vasyl Tasiv had come out in 1892 with only $40. Now he owned a house in Winnipeg, two cows, and had $120 in the bank. Yurko Paish had managed to send $120 home – a small fortune. Dmytro Widynovich had arrived with $40 in 1893 and already had been able to save $400, an enormous sum at a time when an all-wool suit could be purchased for four dollars, and a three-course meal in a restaurant cost no more than twenty-five cents.

It was easy to borrow money. In a town of twenty houses there were three banks, all eager to lend it. You could buy a machine on time. The problem, the professor saw, was not how to borrow money, but how to stop from borrowing too much and going into debt. This was an optimistic country. People talked only of success. Nobody thought of failure.

And yet he was a bit embarrassed by his countrymen.

They seemed to him to be dressed in rags. They didn't appear to bathe and that offended him. He was convinced that newcomers must not look and act like serfs! They would have to wear suits that would cover their bare chests. They must get rid of hooks and ribbons in favour of real buttons. They would have to scrub themselves regularly. They must learn to use a knife and fork. And above all, they would have to get rid of the stigma of slavery. They had to learn to lift their heads and look squarely into the eyes of

Dr. Josef Oleskow visits a small Western Canadian community.

others – instead of peering up from under their brows like dogs.

The professor, of course, was looking for perfection, or at least *his* idea of perfection. It was his dream to turn these Ruthenian peasants into instant Canadian farmers, using Canadian farming techniques, wearing Canadian clothes, and speaking Canadian English. This was a magic vision. The professor would not be the only one who would hold it.

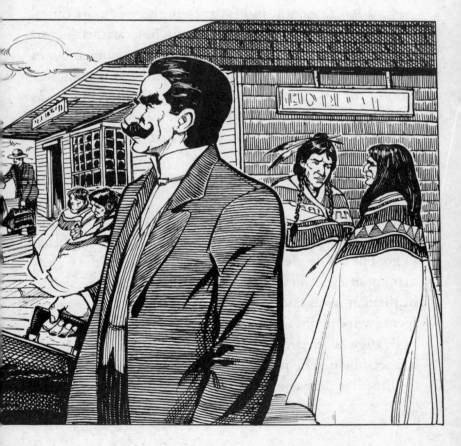

He was shocked during a visit to one farm of Ruthenian colonists. Why, the children seemed to be clothed in filthy cast-offs! As for the women – they didn't even bother to wear blouses.

"For heaven's sake," he cried. "How could you let yourselves go like this?"

To which one woman gave a perfectly sensible answer. She said, "And why not? There is no one to dress for."

But then it must be remembered that Dr. Oleskow had never been a peasant. In his dark suit, he was more out of place than his countrymen. He was a scholar with a doctorate in botany, chemistry, and geology. He was a member of the faculty of the teachers' college in Lemberg – in that section of the old Austro-Hungarian Empire then known as Ruthenia. He was paid $600 a year – an enormous sum for those times and those places. He wanted to better the conditions of the peasantry, partly by improving the mineral and chemical content of the soil, but also by reducing the population through emigration.

But he didn't want his countrymen to set off for the jungles of Brazil, as so many had. That was the wrong place to go. His whole idea was to redirect the flow to the Canadian prairies. And secondly, he wanted to prevent the Ruthenian emigrants from being cheated by crooked agents working for the major shipping companies.

Brazil was offering some goodies – free travel, free land, financial help. The peasants in Ruthenia actually believed the Brazilian propaganda, which suggested they could lie at their ease, while monkeys came down from the trees to do all the work. In fact, those who reached Brazil were treated little better than slaves.

The steamboat agents were a real problem. They were paid extra money for every ticket they sold. They fooled each emigrant in a dozen ways. They charged huge sums to exchange money, took huge fees for fake medical examinations, and bribed the petty officials to ignore their swindles. That explains why these Slavic peasants often arrived in Canada without any money at all.

Dr. Oleskow wanted to change all that. There were too many people in Ruthenia, and as a result wages were very low. There were, in fact, two *million* people too many. But the exploitation of the unschooled emigrants had to be stopped, and that is why the Ruthenian Population Society had sent Dr. Oleskow to Canada.

Dr. Oleskow went to the federal government in Ottawa and announced he was prepared to quit his university post and help control all emigration from Ruthenia and its provinces of Galicia and Bukovina (both part of the modern Ukraine). He didn't want to be paid; he would do it as a labour of love. He wanted to plan a well-organized movement, separate from the steamship companies and their agents. He wanted to choose his people carefully – farmers who had some money and who could be protected from exploitation. These people would be the best stock that Eastern Europe could offer.

Alas, Josef Oleskow was a man ahead of his time. The

government was interested, but cautious. It had already had its share of crackpot idealists. The civil servants knew that Oleskow was not a crackpot, but they were worried about setting a precedent.

Then, in 1896, the government changed. The Conservatives were defeated and the Liberals, under Sir Wilfrid Laurier, came into power. An active new minister, Clifford Sifton, took over the Department of Immigration. But unfortunately Oleskow's scheme did not meet with any enthusiasm from the Austrian government. And the land-owning nobility, who controlled that government, wanted to keep the labour force high and the wages low. Any loss of population would affect them.

Oleskow grew dejected. Thousands read his pamphlets describing the wonders of the Canadian West and planned to leave. But it was the shipping agents who profited. They slipped into the villages disguised as pedlars and signed up anybody they could, promising the moon and cheating their victims.

Oleskow's plan was never adopted. Instead, in 1900, Clifford Sifton decided that almost anyone who had the means to get to Canada would be let in. By that time Oleskow's little trickle of new arrivals had become a tidal wave. For better or worse, his report on the West, in the pamphlet that thousands read, had started a chain reaction.

By 1903, the Galicians, as they were then called (we know them as Poles and Ukrainians today), were strung out by the tens of thousands along the northern rim of the prairies. Josef Oleskow went back to his home and became the director of a teachers' college. But he was gravely ill. On October 18, 1903, the man who helped start it all, but who would soon be forgotten, was dead at the age of forty-three.

Clifford Sifton, the most powerful politician in Western Canada.

CHAPTER TWO

Clifford Sifton's campaign

MORE THAN ANYBODY ELSE, one man is identified with the great tidal wave of Eastern Europeans who poured into the Canadian prairies in the years before the First World War. He was a powerful politician named Clifford Sifton, whose strengths and flaws were as impressive as his strapping six-foot (1.8 m) figure.

Sifton's name will always be connected with a series of dramatic images – the grimy immigrant ships crammed with strange, dark-featured farmers; the colonist cars, crowded with kerchiefed women and men in coats of rough sheepskin; the hovels grubbed out of tough prairie sod; the covered wagons lumbering across the border from the United States; the babel of tongues in Winnipeg's immigration hall; the bell tents of the English colonists whitening the plains of Saskatoon; the gaggle of barefooted Doukhobor fanatics tramping down the frosted roads of Saskatchewan.

Sifton held the post of Minister of the Interior in Wilfrid Laurier's cabinet. His goal was clear. He intended to fill up the West with practical farmers – and nobody else. He didn't want city people, clerks, shopkeepers, or artisans. He didn't want southern Mediterranean people, such as Italians or Spanish. He certainly didn't want Jews, for he claimed (quite wrongly, as the State of Israel was to demonstrate) that Jews didn't make good farmers.

He was convinced that the northern races were the ones who were best for the Canadian West. Scots, Scandinavians, Germans, and British would make excellent citizens. He even thought the northern English would be better than the southern English. He actually paid a higher price to those steamship agents who got people to emigrate from northern England. And the northern Slavs – Poles, Ukrainians and all others identified in those early days as "Galicians" – were welcomed.

Canada was more realistic and also more cautious than the United States, which had welcomed the masses of Europe to its shores, confident in the belief that, once established, they couldn't help but flourish as Americans. Canada wanted only those who wouldn't cost the taxpayers any money.

The Americans saw their country as a home for the downtrodden. Canada really didn't want the downtrodden because they couldn't contribute to the wealth of the nation.

It could be said that, while most emigrants set off for the United States in *search* of something vaguely called the American Dream, the ones who came to Canada were escaping from something that might be called the European nightmare. The Americans offered liberty. The Canadians offered something more practical: free land.

Everybody who arrived in the Northwest was entitled to choose a quarter section – 160 acres (65 hectares) of public land. All he had to do was pay a $10 registration fee. He would have to live on that land and do a certain amount of work on it for three years. If he could stick it out, the land was his.

But before Canada could convince anybody to take up land, some facts about this strange and unkown realm at the top of North America would have to be broadcast.

First, they had to get rid of the image of the West as a snow-covered desert. In Ireland a respected journal was warning people to stay away from Canada because, it said, Manitoba was "a kind of Siberia." One of Sifton's first moves was to prevent anybody publishing the Manitoba temperatures, but he gave that up because it might prove even more alarming.

However, snow was never mentioned in the pamphlets that his department issued. "Cold" was another taboo word. The weather was described as "bracing" and "invigorating." One pamphlet, in fact, said it was so mild that "the soft maple" could grow five feet (1.5 m) in a single season! And if the prospective immigrants confused the Manitoba maple, a weed tree, with the eastern hardwood – Canada's symbol – well, that was too bad.

In his anti-cold campaign, Sifton had the enthusiastic

support of the CPR's colourful chairman, William Cornelius Van Horne, who never lost an opportunity to suggest that the prairies were close to being sub-tropical. He once made a speech in Europe in which he announced that the coldest weather he'd ever known was in Rome and Florence. "I pine for Winnipeg to thaw me," he said. "The atmosphere in the far West intoxicates you, it is so very invigorating" – and he said it with a straight face!

But there were better lures than the weather. Canada was advertised not only as a free country, but also an orderly one. No one needed to carry a gun in the Canadian West. The Mounted Police were establishing an international reputation in the Yukon and they would see to that.

Also the land was free. In addition to your free quarter section, you could usually pick up an adjoining quarter section for a song. Anybody willing to work in the West could make money. The titles of the government pamphlets told the story: *The Wondrous West; Canada, Land of Opportunity; Prosperity Follows Settlement.*

In the first year – 1896 – Sifton's department sent out sixty-five thousand pamphlets. By 1900 the number had reached one million. The best known appeared just after he left office. In thirty-three pages of large type, *The Last and Best West* played on the American myth that praised the farmer as the finest type of citizen. It echoed the legend that the most successful men "have as a rule been those whose youth was spent on a farm."

Sifton took direct charge of this propaganda. One very

successful pamphlet was made up of a series of letters taken from thousands collected by the department from farmers praising the West. The pamphlets were optimistic, but they never indulged in exaggeration.

What kind of a man was Sifton? Certainly he had the reputation of being an iron man, who "never gets tired, works like a horse, never worries, eats three square meals a day, and at night could go to sleep on a nail keg." He had the reputation of staying up all night at his desk leaving behind a pile of work for clerks at six in the morning. He would return to work at ten, looking as fresh as ever. It wasn't just his iron constitution – he had an iron will.

But as his workload increased, his health began to suffer and he was subject to several breakdowns. The strain was increased by his own chronic deafness. He used an ear trumpet, but that didn't help. That inability to hear properly gave him the reputation of being cold, aloof, even ruthless. It was not easy to be close with him. Certainly he didn't suffer fools. He was ambitious and self-assured. He made enemies but he never complained, never explained.

A strong Methodist, he never drank, though that didn't prevent him from passing out gallons of whiskey to his supporters at election time. He was suspicious of Roman Catholics and French Canadians and didn't employ any Quebeckers in his department. Nor did he mingle with his French-Canadian colleagues. That sprang from the traditional Methodism of southern Ontario where the Siftons grew up.

As a politician he had few equals. He was a gold medalist when he graduated from a Methodist college in Cobourg in 1880. He started out adult life as a lawyer, but soon became a politician. By 1890 he was Attorney General of Manitoba. He was a skilled organizer and a tough campaigner. He loved politics with a joy of the battle. They called him the Young Napoleon of the West, after the famous French emperor.

He ran his campaigns like an army general. He had his own intelligence agents. His spies in the opposing camp revealed his opponents' tactics. If he found that they were doing anything illegal or improper, he took them to court.

He was a good speaker – he'd been a Methodist lay preacher in his youth – "the greatest combination of cold-blooded businessman, machine politician and statesman our country has produced," in the words of a man who knew him well.

He was more than a cabinet minister. He was in charge of the Liberal political machine in the West, totally in control of party propaganda, party patronage, and election tactics.

"The men in sheepskin coats," as Sifton dubbed them, later became his loyal supporters. He made every effort to convince them that it was the Liberal government that had brought them to the promised land. He virtually dictated the texts of political pamphlets that were designed to convince the newcomers to vote for his party.

Even the smallest ethnic groups received his attention.

There were about forty Icelandic voters in Manitoba in 1900, but Sifton went after all of them, bringing in speakers of Icelandic descent to spread the Liberal gospel. He even put one Icelandic youth in the local post office after he learned that the clerk, who couldn't tell one Icelander from another, had been blindly handing out Liberal campaign literature to the Conservatives. And of course he found jobs for good Liberals but not for good Tories, the "nickname" for the Conservatives.

He was not only the most powerful political figure in the Canadian West, but when he bought the *Manitoba Free Press* (later the *Winnipeg Free Press*) in the winter of 1898-99, he became the most powerful journalist. It had its advantages and disadvantages for the country. But it had a great advantage for the poor and dispossessed people of Eastern Europe who arrived in the new country bewildered and unsure of themselves. A great many newspapers were hostile to the newcomers. Sifton's paper tried to tell the other side of the story and thus gave a measure of hope to the men and women in sheepskin coats.

CHAPTER THREE

The ordeal of the Galicians

IN THE MOUNTAIN TRENCHES of Galicia, the land was too precious to be wasted. The furrows of the strip farms ran to the very edges of the houses. Cows and sheep dotted the pasture land on the lower sides of the mountains. Oats, rye, and potatoes sprouted up from the valley floor. Above the huddle of thatched roofs the great mountain peaks rose, covered in oak, beech, and fir, each ridge effectively sealing one village from the next, preserving a peasant way of life that was frozen in time.

Since there were no fences – only corner stakes to mark personal holdings – each fertile Carpathian valley resembled one gigantic farm under a single management. But appearances were deceptive. Each peasant needed fourteen acres (5.6 hectares) to provide for himself and his family, and yet seventy percent of the farms were no more than half that size. In fact, some families' wages were as low as five cents a day, while the price of land, for those who could afford it, was high. Land, in fact, fetched as much as $400 an acre. Taxes were also among the highest in Europe.

Under these depressing conditions, theft was common and alcoholism universal. The wealthy lords owned not only the forests, meadows, and villages, but also the taverns – there were more twenty-three thousand of these in Galicia. It was in the interests of the ruling class to keep the peasants drunk and underpaid. The consumption of liquor was almost unbelievable – twenty-six litres a year for every man, woman, and child.

Let us look into the Galician village of Ghermakivka on a spring morning in 1897, a year after the Sifton immigration policy went into high gear. The Humeniuk family is packing to leave for Canada on money borrowed from relatives and friends. Everything the Humeniuks own takes up no more than twenty cubic feet (0.6 cu. m.). It is carefully stored away in a green wooden trunk built by Nykola Humeniuk himself.

His wife, Anastasia, puts the winter clothes, blankets, and bedsheets at the bottom. Then come the holy pictures, packed between pillows. On top of that are the family's dress clothes for Sunday church. For the emigrants are certain there will be a little church with an onion-shaped spire in whatever community they may reach.

On top of that there is another covering, and then twenty-five little cloth bundles of garden seeds – onions, garlic, horseradish, dried ears of corn. Above that, some religious articles – candles, chalk, a bottle of holy water. Four precious books will also be taken: a prayer book, a history of the Ukraine, a school primer, and a collection of

Bible stories. And, finally, Nykola's carpentry and farm tools: hammers and planes, axe and draw-knife, saws, bits, chisels, sickles, scythes, hoes, a rake, and flail.

At last the task is done. Anastasia ties up some food for the trip in a cloth bundle. The neighbours and relatives pour into the house to say goodbye. Everybody is talking at once. There are smiles at first, then suddenly some of the women begin to cry. They hug and kiss Anastasia, apologizing for things left undone and past offences, real and imagined. The children start to cry too. Then some of the men are seen to wipe tears from their eyes.

Somebody shouts for silence. Then, as all bow their heads, he begins to recite a prayer, asking God to bless the family and their two small children, Pettryk and baby Theodore, and to give them a safe voyage, prosperity, and good health in the strange land across the ocean. Write soon, everybody cries, write as soon as you arrive!

The wagon and team are waiting for the journey to the station. Four men hoist the big trunk onto the back as the family climbs aboard. But Anastasia Humeniuk stops and turns back, her baby in her arms. She walks to the doorway, makes the sign of the cross, kisses the frame, and then, in one last gesture, picks up a small lump of Galician earth, wraps it in a rag, and puts it in her hand valise, a memory of a land she will never see again.

Professor Oleskow's plan had been to bring to Canada only the best farmers – the most productive and educated elements – people who owned enough land to finance the long journey and the first years on the Canadian homestead. But that plan was never acted on. The steamship agents, to whom each peasant paid a fee, wanted to sign up as many as possible. And so it was the ignorant and the innocent, like the Humeniuks, who came to Canada and were exploited shamelessly by those who stood to make a profit from them.

There are many examples of this. Let's look at the little Galician town of Oswiecim, now a part of Poland. There, two immigration agents, Jacob Klausner and Simon Herz, were masters at the art of bribery and corruption. They paid off all the local officials, including both the police and the railway conductors, in order to get as many people under their control as possible.

They overcharged shamelessly for ocean passage. They cheated on the exchange rate. They sold worthless advertising cards instead of tickets. If a man was the right age for compulsory military service and thus unable to emigrate legally, they charged double to smuggle him out of the country. And whenever anybody was foolish enough to object, he was locked into a barn and beaten.

There were other swindles. One Polish agent invented a fake telephone on which he received fake "information." It was only an alarm clock. However, when it rang, he claimed it was inquiring about passage. And when the clock rang again, he charged the peasant a special fee for its use. Sometimes he'd used the clock to ask "the American emperor," whether he'd allow the hopeful emigrant to enter Canada. That, of course, meant another fee.

One swindler dressed up as a doctor and pretended to fail emigrants. Then he would accept a bribe and pass them on. Another had a store full of clothing that he sold at high prices, claiming the peasants wouldn't be allowed to wear their native dress in Canada. At the ocean ports, especially in Germany, scores were told they would have to wait for a boat. They would be deliberately held in boarding houses, hotels, and taverns, where they were cheated for lodgings and food.

One group from Bukovina arrived at Winnipeg's immigration hall in May 1897 protesting that everything had been misrepresented to them. They'd been told that the "Crown Princess of Austria" was in Montreal and would see they were given free land with houses, cattle, and farm equipment. All they had to do was telegraph her if these promises went unfulfilled. As a result many refused all offers of jobs in Winnipeg and sat in the crowded immigration hall. With five hundred more newcomers arriving, the police attempted to move them out. A small riot ensued. Many were flung to the floor and were then dragged or carried off, the women yelling and shrieking.

The former mayor of Winnipeg, William McCreary, was now the immigration commissioner in Winnipeg. He had been working from six in the morning till nine at night, getting a special low rate on the railway to Yorkton for the immigrants. He'd also arranged for fifty days' work for those who were destitute. But that didn't suit the new arrivals. They had been fooled by the steamship agents' promises and so refused to board the train. Some upset the baggage carts. Some, with their goods on their backs, started marching north. Others squatted on the street or seized vacant houses near the track. In the end, of course, they gave in.

McCreary got them some flour and a few bushels of potatoes and finally settled them on homesteads in the vicinity of Saltcoats, Assiniboia, near Yorkton, where eventually they forgot about the non-existent Austrian princess. It was exactly this kind of fraud and exploitation that Professor Oleskow had wished to avoid.

It is understandable that so many immigrants were saddened and rebellious when they reached this country. Apart from the false promises, there was a long journey across Europe from their home villages, and then the stormy ocean voyage in the holds of the immigrant ships. Once they left home, the first stop, usually after a twenty-four-hour train journey, came at a control station between Galicia and Germany. There, everybody had to submit to a medical examination before going further. These stations had been set up after a cholera epidemic in 1892 and were run by the steamship companies. Now everybody coming into Germany from Austria-Hungary or from Russia en route to North America had to take a medical exam.

So let's look at one of these control stations at Myslowitz at the junction of the German, Austrian, and Russian borders. A uniformed official leads the people from the Krakow train through a long hall to a desk behind which stand three more officials: a steamship agent and, in uniform, a Russian policeman and a German officer. The immigrants give up their rail and steamship tickets to the agent, and then, clutching their baggage, are led into two large halls where the Galicians are separated from the Russians.

This hall has a tiled floor, painted walls, a high ceiling, and windows of coloured glass. It is ringed by wooden benches, under which they stuff their baggage. As many as can find space sleep on the benches; the rest stretch out on baggage or on the floor, men, women, and children all crammed together. The walls are alive with lice.

No one is allowed to leave until the next train arrives. The only available food is sold at a canteen, but the canteen keeper is drunk, and, in spite of a long price list on the wall, the stock consists mainly of beer, wine, and liquor, but no tea or coffee.

More officers arrive with more immigrants. The first immigrants ask for breakfast but are told only the canteen can supply it. At nine, the wife of the canteen keeper turns up and makes some coffee. At noon, for twenty-five cents, they get a dinner of soup, boiled beef, potato salad, and bread. Many can't afford it.

At two in the afternoon a doctor arrives. The immigrants have been waiting almost twenty-four hours to be inspected; others wait much longer. They are driven into another room, pass in single file before the doctor, and wait for their clothing and baggage to be disinfected.

Their tickets are returned and they are packed aboard the train, faced with a twenty-four-hour journey across Germany. The third-class coach is so crowded that many have to stand for all that time. And at Hamburg there is another medical inspection.

At this point, those who have paid steerage fees – for the cheapest accommodations – are told there is no more room on the ship. They will have to wait another ten days, or pay an additional thirty marks for a third-class ticket. Some can't afford the extra fare or the cost of waiting. Cheated by agents, who lied to them that their rail fare had been paid in advance, they have already spent their meagre funds. They can't even afford to send a telegram home.

Now a flurry of counting, consulting, borrowing, and lending takes place as the immigrants pool their money, decide to pay the extra fare, and set off across the angry ocean, gambling that they won't be rejected on the other side for lack of funds.

For most, the ocean voyage was a nightmare. Jammed into tiered bunks in stifling holds of ancient vessels, vomiting from sea sickness, half-starved, and terror-stricken by hurricane-force gales, men, women, and children were flung together under conditions that made a mockery of privacy.

But that was not the real horror. It was the storms that raged on the Atlantic that drove them to a state of terror. One of these immigrants, Theodore Nemerski, has left a graphic account of his own experiences on the *Christiana* in the spring of 1896. He was one of the first Galicians to be influenced by Professor Oleskow's pamphlet. Now, here he was, with eight other members of his family. Four days out of port, the storm broke.

"Good Lord! What fear grips one here. You look, and here from the side there appears a great opening. The water has drawn back and the whole ship simply flies into that void, turning almost completely over on its side. And here all of a sudden a huge mountain with a great roar and clatter of the waves tears into the ship, spilling over the top onto the other side. This is no place to be! ... escape inside.

"Inside you find complete panic ... all are silent ... whispering prayers ... awaiting the end ...

"Some tied their eyes so as not to see this terror, while they hung onto the bed so they would not fall out. Suddenly water is coming in to the inside from the top, splashing from wall to wall. The people are in lament. Some cry, some complain: Did we need this? It was good for us to live in the old country. This is all on account of you ... I listened to you and now we shall all perish ...."

On the *Arcadia,* another ancient ship carrying immigrants, the crew herded the passengers below and locked the hatches when the storm struck. Fifteen hundred Galicians clung to the four tiers of iron beds, praying and vomiting, the stench so ghastly that those stewards who ventured in were themselves taken sick.

An old man and a child died before the storm was over. But that was not the end. The ship struck an iceberg. When the hole in the side was repaired, the captain discovered that he was locked in the grip of the frozen ocean and couldn't move. All the passengers were herded back on deck and required to race from side to side – back and forth, back and forth – on signals from the ship's whistle, until the *Arcadia*

For most immigrants to Canada, the ocean voyage from Europe was a nightmare of seasickness, bad food, and cramped quarters.

was finally shaken free from her icy embrace. By this time most of the baggage was soaked and ruined. One month after they left their home villages, the hapless passengers finally landed at Quebec City on the St. Lawrence River.

For those who were able to eat, the food was generally terrible: filthy water, rotten herrings, dirty potatoes, rancid lard, smelly meat – all eaten from unwashed dishes and cutlery. The staple meat was pork – not the best remedy for a sick stomach. Thirty years later after his ordeal, one immigrant wrote: "To this moment I cannot face the warm smell of pork without sweat starting on my forehead."

Another, who travelled steerage on the *Bavaria* in 1904, claimed that he was served pig's feet three times a day and "had visions of millions of pigs being sacrificed so that their feet could be given to the many emigrants leaving Europe."

The more fortunate travelled third class, which was a bit better than steerage, although it did no more than provide decently for the simplest human needs. As one woman put it, "to travel in anything worse than what is offered in the third class is to arrive at the journey's end with a mind unfit for healthy, wholesome impressions and with a body weakened and unfit for the hardships that are involved in the beginning of life in a new land."

Yet tens of thousands of sturdy men, women, and children, who quit their tiny Carpathian farms to make a new life in a world of strangers, endured it all and somehow managed to survive and prosper.

CHAPTER FOUR

"Ignorant, foreign scum"

As one might expect, the Galicians who arrived in Halifax in Nova Scotia or Quebec City after a month of hard travel presented a sorry and bedraggled appearance. Few had any idea of distance. They'd never, until this moment, gone more than twenty-five or thirty miles (40 to 48 km) from their homes. They didn't realize the need for changes of clothing. Everything was packed away in trunks, boxes, and valises, to be opened only when they reached their prairie homes.

It's important to realize that these were a people obsessed with cleanliness, used to scrubbing themselves regularly. Now, suffering from a lack of washing facilities on train and steamship, they looked and felt unclean.

Maria Olinyk, a nine-year-old girl from the western Ukraine, later remembered how the crowd on the dock at Halifax stared at her and her shipmates, some out of curiosity, some out of contempt. Here were women in peasant costumes, and men in coats of strong-smelling sheepskin wearing fur hats, linen blouses, and trousers tucked into enormous boots, their long hair greased with lard. The

Canadians, Maria noticed, stopped their noses. These first impressions of the newcomers helped to encourage the wave of anti-Galician feeling that was fed by the anti-Sifton newspapers.

Thus Sir Mackenzie Bowell, a former Conservative prime minister and leader of his party in the Senate, was able to write in his newspaper, the Belleville *Intelligencer*, that "the Galicians, they of the sheepskin coats, the filth and the vermin do not make splendid material for the building of a great nation. One look at the disgusting creatures after they pass through over the CPR on their way West has caused many to marvel that beings bearing the human form could have sunk to such a bestial level...."

To many newcomers, the new land, at first glimpse, seemed equally appalling. Dmytro Romanchych, who came out from the mountains of Bukovina as a result of reading Professor Oleskow's pamphlet, never forgot his first sight of Quebec City – streaks of dirty grey snow lying in the ravines. The sad, uninviting landscape made him feel that Canada was sparsely settled and inhospitable. Dmytro felt depressed, for he had left a land whose meadows and glens, three weeks before, had been green with the promise of early spring. Ottawa with its granite Parliament buildings was more impressive, but across the river the land seemed wild, with the bare rock banks and sickly trees making an unpleasant impression.

But these vistas were cheerful compared to the despair that seized the newcomers when the colonist trains rattled and swayed across the Precambrian desert of the Canadian

Shield in northern Ontario. Theodore Nemerski, barely recovered from the storm that tore at the *Christiana,* was shaken by the possibility that this broken expanse of granite ridges and stunted pines might in fact be the actual promised land that Oleskow had described. His companions "turned grey with fear." What if there were no better soil than this in Canada? they asked. "Here the heart froze in not a few men ... the hair on the head stands on end ... because not a few think, what if they get into something like this?"

This was not an unusual attitude. When the Humeniuk family came out the following year, 1897, the women in their car began to sob and cry out that "it would have been better to suffer in the old country than to come to this Siberia." Two years later Maria Olinyk felt the same shock of apprehension. "The heart of many a man sank to his heels," she remembered, "and the women and the children raised such lamentations as defies description."

There were other problems. In Montreal, the Galicians were met by hordes of small-time hustlers trying to separate them from their funds, charging high prices for food, hawking useless goods, and urging them not to venture farther west. The situation became so serious in the spring of 1897 that immigration authorities were forced to call in the police and confine the new arrivals to sheds, until they could be put into railway cars with their final destination clearly marked and the tickets in their hands.

The exploitation resumed in Winnipeg, the jumping-off

spot for the prairies. Here, a group of Winnipeg real estate agents collared six Galicians, discovered they had twelve thousand dollars among them, and talked them out of leaving Winnipeg. They claimed it was too cold in Alberta and that the very horns on the cattle froze in the winter. The real estate men were a little too persuasive. Four of their victims immediately bought tickets and returned to Europe.

There were other disappointments. Maria Olinyk and her family were among those who took one of the special trains to the Yorkton area where hundreds of their fellow countrymen were homesteading. A friend who had come out the year before had written to them, boasting of his prosperity, describing his home as a mansion, telling of his immense cultivated fields and how his wife now dressed like a lady. He depicted Canada "as a country of incredible abundance whose borders were braided with sausage like some fantastic land in a fairy tale."

The family hired a rig and after a thirty-mile (48 km) journey north through clouds of mosquitoes finally reached their destination. What they found was a small log cabin, partially plastered and roofed with sod, a tiny garden plot dug with a spade, a woman dressed in ancient torn overalls "suntanned like a gypsy," and her husband, his face smeared with dirt from ear to ear, "weird, like some unearthly creature," grubbing up stumps. Maria's mother broke into tears at the sight, but, like so many others, the Olinyk family hung on and, after years of pain and hardship, eventually prospered. Maria became Dr. Maria

Adamowska, a noted Ukrainian-Canadian poet who, when she died in 1961 at Melville, Saskatchewan, left behind a literary legacy that included her vivid memories of those lean, far-off years.

The Galicians did not care to settle on the bald southern prairie. They preferred the wooded valleys of the Saskatchewan River. This baffled the immigration authorities. "These Galicians are a peculiar people," McCreary wrote to Sifton's deputy minister, James Smart, in the spring of 1897. "They will not accept as a gift 160 acres of what we consider the best land in Manitoba, that is first class wheat growing prairie land; what they particularly want is wood; and they care but little whether the land is heavy soil or light gravel; but each man must have some wood on his place...."

There was a reason for this. Wood was precious in the Carpathians – so scarce that it was bought by the pound. In some areas the harvesting of wood was a monopoly; it was a crime to cut down a tree. Thus in Canada the Galicians were allowed, perhaps even encouraged, to settle on marginal lands while other immigrants, notably the Americans, seized the more fertile prairie to the south.

Let us, once again, follow the fortunes of the Humeniuk family whom we saw leaving Galicia some weeks before. They arrived in Winnipeg in June of 1897. In the colonist car they sat quietly on their seats as they had been told, peering curiously out of the windows at the equally curious crowd on the platform peering in. Suddenly they spotted a

Newcomers piled into colonist cars which rattled their way across the Canadian Shield and prairies.

familiar figure – a Galician searching about for acquaintances. His name was Michaniuk and he soon spotted his old friends.

"Neighbours!" Mr. Michaniuk shouted, "where are you going?"

There was a commotion in the car. Where *were* they going? Nobody seemed to know. "Don't go any farther!" cried Mr. Michaniuk to his former townspeople. "It is good here!"

One of the men in the coach rose to his feet and addressed the assembly.

"This is our neighbour, Mr. Michaniuk. He came to Canada last year. He says it is good here. Let us get off the train."

A stampede took place. Men seized the doors, but found them to be locked. They tried the windows, but those were fastened too. Several, in a frenzy, picked up their handbags, smashed the glass, and began to crawl through the openings, throwing their goods ahead of them. The Humeniuk family was carried forward by the press of people onto the platform.

A conductor ran up with an interpreter.

"What are you going to do now?" the interpreter cried. "We have good land for you near Yorkton. There are no free good homesteads for farming left in Manitoba."

But the newcomers could not be convinced. A spokesman replied: "We are not going any farther. Our old country friend has been here one year. He says it's good where he settled."

Nobody could persuade them to go on to Yorkton. They

were moved to the immigration hall where the women began to cook food, to launder the clothes, and to tend to the children. The men followed Mr. Michaniuk to the Dominion Land Office to file for homesteads near Stuartburn on the Roseau River, near the American border, where thirty-seven Galician families were already located.

It turned out that some land was still available and it was there that they settled. Most of them were still there a half a century later, when Nykola and Anastasia Humeniuk, surrounded by grandchildren, celebrated their golden wedding anniversary on the farm they filed for back in 1897.

The sheepskin people had to make do with essentials. Their homes were built of timber and whitewashed clay, the roofs thatched with straw. Whole families slept on top of the vast stove-furnaces six feet (1.8 m) square. Gardens were dug with spades because they couldn't afford better equipment. Benches and tables were handmade. Plates were hammered out of tin cans found in garbage dumps. Drinking glasses were created by cutting a beer bottle in half.

Browbeaten for centuries, the Galicians didn't find it easy to throw off old habits. W.A. Griesbach, the young mayor of Edmonton, found them timid and frightened and noticed that when a uniformed policeman approached, they drove right off the road, removed their caps, and waited for him to go by. If a well-dressed Canadian gave them an order they would immediately obey. This made them ripe targets for exploitation.

One man who worked with them on the railway

described them as "naïve, trustful, bearded giants [who] worked like elephants, laughed like children and asked no questions," but were subject to "ruthless, brazen robbery." The food was meagre and barely edible; better fare was available in the company's store, but "for prices that New York night clubs would be ashamed to ask.... Those who didn't like it could get out (at their own expense) for there was a never ending stream shanghaied by the mass-procurement agencies of the East.... The Ukrainians were held in check by the small Anglo-Saxon element present in every camp, who, being decently treated, were always ready to put down with fists, clubs, and even guns, any outbreak of the 'Bohunks.'"

All the same, the newcomers were changing the look of the prairies. Carpathian villages with neat, whitewashed houses and thatched roofs sprang up. Onion-shaped spires began to dominate the landscape. Mingled with the silhouettes of the grain elevators, and the familiar style of the prairie railway stations, they helped create a profile that was distinctively Western.

To those public figures who had no axe to grind, they were an attractive addition to the prairie mix. William Van Horne, president of the CPR, found them "a very desirable people." Charles Constantine, a veteran mounted policeman at Fort Saskatchewan, used the same adjective. The immigration agent in Edmonton said, "They are settlers, and I should like to see more of them."

Van Horne, in 1899, was astonished to discover that those who had been given railway transportation on credit actually paid the money back. As he said, "We had little hope of ever getting what they owed us, but they paid up every cent." And several who had first opposed their arrival changed their minds.

One doctor described his visit to a Galician colony as "a revelation." He described the colonists as "worthy, industrious, sober, and ambitious to make homes for themselves."

Another who also changed his mind was W.M. Fisher of the Canada Permanent Mortgage Company, who reported that "the Galicians against whom I was prejudiced before my visit... I found to be a most desirable class of settler, being hard working, frugal people and in their financial dealings honest to a degree."

The attitude of the newspapers was predictable. The government papers thought they were wonderful; the opposition papers thought the opposite. The first wave had scarcely stepped ashore when the Conservative papers mounted a vicious attack. To the Belleville *Intelligencer* they were "disgusting creatures," to the Brandon *Independent* "human vermin." The Ottawa *Citizen* objected to Canada "being turned into a social sewage farm to purify the rinsings and leavings of rotten European states." In Edmonton, the *Bulletin* pulled out all the stops. It said the Galicians were "a servile, shiftless people ... the scum of other lands ... not a people who are wanted in this country at any price."

The attacks were entirely political. In the pro-Sifton newspapers, the Galicians could do no wrong. But the public outcry by the Conservatives in Parliament finally forced Sifton to put a damper on Galician immigration. The general belief was that the influx of Slavs would dilute and muddy the purity of Canada's Anglo-Saxon heritage.

Hugh John Macdonald, the son of Canada's first prime minister, actually referred to the Galicians as "a mongrel race." Premier Roblin of Manitoba went farther. He called them "foreign trash" and proceeded to deny them the vote in order to "defend the 'old flag' against an invading foe."

The Conservatives harped on the belief that these Galicians were sub-humans with violent criminal tendencies, subject to greed and uncontrollable passions. Mackenzie Bowell wrote of "tales of murder, arson and brutality, more horrible than anything ever dreamed of by the wildest disciple of the school of realistic fiction." These were not the words of a street-corner bigot – they came from the pen of a former prime minister.

We have heard the same comments in our own time, especially in those areas where emigrants from the Far East have also been attacked, without evidence, as criminals, thieves, and wife-beaters.

The tales of the Galicians were simple fiction. One newspaper, the Shoal Lake *Star,* wrote of murder, robbery, wife-beating, and other crimes being committed among the Galicians in that area. But when Wesley Speers, of the Immigration Department, went to Shoal Lake and tracked down every story, he found them all to be untrue. He forced an apology from the newspaper, and a correction.

Yet the concept of the Galicians as potentially dangerous criminals stayed in the public mind. That was because every Galician who got into trouble was identified in bold headlines. "GALICIAN HORROR" is the way the *Winnipeg Daily Tribune* headlined a local murder in June of 1899, convicting the man out of hand long before he went to trial.

Another Galician charged with murder was castigated before his trial as "an inhuman wretch." Trial by newspapers was far more common at the turn of the century than it is today. The following month the pro-Conservative Winnipeg *Telegram* reported the murder of Mrs. Robert Lane of Brandon in July of 1895, identifying her assailant as Galician. It titled its story as "ANOTHER SIFTONIAN TRAGEDY." It said that "In order that Mr. Sifton may keep his Liberal party in power by the votes of ignorant and vicious foreign scum he is dumping on our prairies, we are to submit to have our nearest and dearest butchered on our door-steps."

The entire story was a lie. The murderer wasn't a Galician, but an English woman who confessed to the crime and hanged for it. But the impression of Galician madmen murdering defenseless Canadian women was hard to erase.

As for real Galician crime, it hardly existed. That same year, the chief of police in Winnipeg released annual figures showing the ethnic origins of convicted prisoners. Of 1,205 criminals, 1,037 were Canadians, and 168 were foreign born, and of these latter, only *nine* were Galicians.

B Y 1904, THE ATTITUDE towards the sheepskin people had begun to change, and for a very practical reason. The newspapers and politicians who had attacked "Sifton's dirty Slavs" reversed themselves. The violently Tory Winnipeg *Telegram,* for instance, which had attacked the immigrants as "ignorant, superstitious and filthy," now discovered that they were "industrious," "thrifty," "progressive," and "prosperous."

The reason was that there was an election, and everybody was scrambling for Galician votes. Even the Tory premier of Manitoba was having second thoughts. He had once called the newcomers "dirty ignorant Slavs" who lived on rats and mice, but now he rose in the legislature to praise "their diligence, their intelligence, their sobriety, their generally estimable character."

They'd been denied the provincial vote in Manitoba back in 1899. Now the premier gave it to them. He had to do something to defeat the federal Liberal campaign which was making such great headway among all the immigrants in the West. Immigrants voted for the Liberals because the

Liberal party had opened the doors to immigrants and given them free land.

It's doubtful whether many really understood the Canadian electoral system. In Europe they had voted for "electors" – one for every five hundred voters – who, in turn, went to the political centre of their district and voted for the actual candidate, usually a big land owner. That system made the newcomers suspicious of all politicians. And that was reinforced when they discovered that in Canada a vote could be sold for a dollar. Some sold their votes twice – once to each opposing candidate, and then voted as they pleased.

Nor could they understand a word the politicians uttered when they toured the villages. Both parties had to use interpreters. There was a story of one interpreter warming up a crowd of potential Liberal voters by telling them, "I'm going to call upon the local candidate to speak, and I want you to listen carefully. When I start clapping I want all of you to do the same. And when he finishes I want all of you to give him a great ovation. You won't regret it and neither will I." And of course he was paid off by the Liberals for that.

Frank Oliver, a Conservative candidate, once spoke to a group of Galicians in a small general store in his riding near Edmonton. Nobody had any idea of what the man was saying, except for the local party interpreter. If they had known they would have had little interest in the subject because he was ranting on about free trade.

"What's he say?" one listener finally asked the interpreter.

Liberal politician Frank Oliver speaks to a group of new Canadians.

"He's glad we're here. Canada was lucky to get us...."

"What about the stupid fire regulations?"

"He'll fix them."

"What's he say about the railroad?"

"I forgot to tell you that – he's got it started for sure."

"What about the mudholes around Whitford Lake?"

"He'll fix them – he'll do all he can for our area.... "

Frank Oliver was not above dressing up some of his supporters as surveyors pretending to drive highways through Galician farmyards in preparation for an apparent new railway. When the despairing immigrant begged for a changed route, the fake surveyors told them to get in touch with the local Liberal agent who might be able to help them. In every case, of course, the Liberals agreed, and the farmer gave Oliver his vote.

The newcomers were also vague about voting dates. Because they didn't read any English an effort was needed to get out the vote, or in some cases to keep the vote away. Oliver had his organizers swarm over the Galician communities asking each man whom he intended to vote for. Those who were voting Liberal were told the proper date of the election was Monday. But the Conservative voters were told it was Wednesday.

It was Oliver who replaced Clifford Sifton the following year as Minister of the Interior. Not surprisingly, the concept of unrestricted immigration was tossed aside when the government changed.

There was no talk about multiculturalism then. The big

word was "assimilation." The people who ran the country wanted conformity – in dress, in language, in customs, in attitudes, and in religion. Every immigrant who arrived in the West was expected to accept as quickly as possible the Anglo-Celtic, Protestant values of his Canadian neighbours.

In those days everybody agreed that certain races couldn't be assimilated and had no place in Canadian society. Orientals, East Indians, and Blacks were not wanted. Anti-Semitism was universal. The press was racist. They called the Blacks niggers, Orientals were Chinamen, and the Jews were sheenies.

Could the Galicians be assimilated or would their presence "mongrelise" the nation when they mixed with other races and groups? That was the basis of the argument from the moment they arrived. It was generally agreed they were an inferior race, but that wasn't the problem. The question was whether or not they could be turned into "white" Canadians.

The anti-Sifton newspapers didn't believe it possible. As the Edmonton *Bulletin,* owned by Frank Oliver, said, "They have withstood assimilation in the country from whence they come for many generations. What reason have we to expect their ready assimilation here?" Others were grudgingly optimistic. As the Hamilton *Times* put it, "They may never develop into such perfect Canadians as the Scotch or the Irish, but the chances are they will turn out all right."

As we know now, they did turn out all right. The son of one of those immigrant families, Ray Hnatyshyn, would one day become Governor General of Canada.

The general sentiment was one of optimism. A new century was dawning – "Canada's century," Prime Minister Wilfrid Laurier called it. It was a country capable of working miracles. The men in sheepskin coats would be quickly transformed into well-cropped, bowler-hatted Canadians – or so it was believed. As the *Manitoba Free Press* put it, "the land is here and the Anglo-Saxon race has great assimilating qualities." To William McCreary, the Galicians were "already dressing in a more civilized garb" and "accepting Canadian customs and ways."

One of several reasons that some leading Canadians wanted the Galicians to assimilate was because they wanted them to be sturdy Protestants, and not Orthodox Catholics. J.W. Sparling, the principal of Winnipeg's Methodist Wesley College, wrote, "there is danger and it is national! Either we must educate and elevate the incoming multitudes or they will drag us and our children down to a lower level. We must see to it that the civilization and ideals of Southeastern Europe are not transplanted to and perpetuated on our virgin soil." In Sparling's view, these ideals, of course, were those of the Catholic religions.

The Methodist publication *Missionary Outlook* summed up the Methodist point of view in 1908, when it wrote: "If from this North American continent is to come a superior race, a race to be specially used of God in the carrying on of

His work, what is our duty to those who are now our fellow-citizens? Many of them come to us as nominal Christians, that is, they owe allegiance to the Greek or Roman Catholic churches but their moral standards and ideals are far below those of the Christian citizens of the Dominion....It is our duty to meet them with an open Bible, and to install into their minds the principles and ideals of Anglo-Saxon civilization."

But nobody asked the Galicians whether or not they wished to be ground up in the great Anglo-Saxon mill. They clung fiercely to their religion. And indeed, the presence of Roman Catholic and Greek Orthodox churches in the rural prairies helped them keep their language and culture. Certainly, many wanted to learn English and wanted their children to learn it. In this desire they were often held back by the lack of good teachers. But they also wanted to keep their original language, and this they did to a remarkable degree, producing an impressive body of prose and poetry in their own tongue.

The fears of "mongrelisation" were groundless. The newcomers and their children managed to become Canadians while retaining a pride in their heritage, as the Scots did, as the Icelanders and others did. By the First World War, when immigration ceased, the talk of assimilation began to subside. By the 1920s, the term "Galician" had died out.

By then, most Canadians were beginning to understand the difference between Poles and Ukrainians, for by then

Polish and Ukrainian social and political clubs were scattered across the West. The time was coming when Canadians of every background would be referring to the Canadian "mosaic" and later to "multiculturalism" and, indeed, boasting about it as if it had been purposely invented as an instrument of national policy to preserve the Dominion from the American Melting Pot.

CHAPTER SIX

~

The Spirit Wrestlers

AT 4 P.M. ON JANUARY 20, 1899 – a perfect winter's day – the S.S. *Lake Huron* steamed into Halifax harbour with twenty-one hundred Doukhobors on board. This was the largest single body of emigrants ever to have crossed the Atlantic in one ship. She had travelled for twenty-nine days from the Black Sea port of Batum, in the Russian district of Georgia, manned by a skeleton crew (to save money).

Ten persons had died during the voyage; five couples had been married in the simple Doukhobor ceremony. The new arrivals had also survived a dreadful tempest that blew unceasingly for eight days, causing all to give up hope of ever reaching Canadian shores. In spite of this, the ship was spanking clean, scrubbed spotless by the women. The chief health officer said he'd never known so clean a vessel to enter Halifax harbour.

These too were people in sheepskin coats, though not known as Galicians. They came from the valleys of the Caucasus Mountains between the Caspian and Black Seas – a religious group who lived communally, rejected military service, and refused to take an oath of allegiance to the Czar. They called themselves the Christian Community of Universal Brotherhood, but their tormenters jeered at them "Doukhoborski," or spirit wrestlers.

The name stuck and in the end was accepted with pride in the same way the Society of Friends accepted the word "Quaker." They came to Canada as a result of money raised by a group of high-minded Canadians and Russian noblemen – including Count Leo Tolstoy, the world-famous author of the novel *War and Peace* – who could not stomach the persecution they were receiving in Russia. They did not come at the invitation of the Canadian government, but there was little the government could do about them. They were coming anyway – twenty-one hundred of them.

Nothing like this had ever taken place before. Somehow all of these people – men, women, and children – scarcely any of whom understood a word of English, had to be taken halfway across Canada as soon as they got off the boat.

How to find shelter in Winnipeg for these new arrivals? Who was going to house twenty-one hundred people? The immigration shed could handle no more than six hundred. The shed at Brandon held no more than four hundred, and that was ice cold, the wind blowing snow and ice through the cracks in the walls.

Nor was the department equipped to feed such an army. William McCreary, the immigration agent, was planning to throw up a frame shed at Yorkton. There was another at Dauphin, Manitoba, which would hold three hundred, mainly women and children. An additional hundred could perhaps be squeezed into the shed at Brandon, another hundred at Birtle, and upward of fifty at Qu'Appelle. That would still leave another hundred who would have to be crowded into the overtaxed hall in Winnipeg.

McCreary was on the verge of a breakdown from overwork. He felt powerless to cope with the Doukhobor influx. He had no authority to buy anything. No committee had been organized to handle the money raised from the Doukhobors themselves and from well-wishers. He had to find wood, water, harnesses, oxen, sleighs, flour, vegetables. He couldn't locate sixty-gallon (272 L) cooking pots in the West – they would have to be shipped by freight, and that would take ten days or longer if there was a blizzard.

Five trainloads of Doukhobors began arriving in Winnipeg at noon on the afternoon of January 27, 1899. This was the coldest winter in the memory of the city's oldest inhabitants! When the third train pulled in, it was one o'clock in the morning, and so cold on the platform that McCreary froze his nose and fingers.

Train No. 4 was an hour behind, en route to Brandon. The fifth train arrived at 5:30 and collided with a yard engine just as it pulled out for Dauphin. Two cars were damaged and had to be replaced.

But the Doukhobors were in a state of near ecstasy. To them, McCreary's makeshift arrangements felt like heaven on earth. Hot dinners awaited them the moment they stepped off the train. The women of Winnipeg had spent hours peeling potatoes and chopping cabbage and making soup. Thousands turned out the following day to greet them.

An address of welcome was offered by a local church minister, heading a committee especially organized for the purpose. There were tears in the eyes of the onlookers when he spoke.

As far as the Spirit Wrestlers were concerned, their problems were over. But McCreary's were just beginning. He'd managed to house two thousand-odd Doukhobors in temporary quarters, but now he was faced with four new concerns. With winter coming on he had to clothe these people, move food out to them, provide real housing, and do this before another two thousand arrived. For they were already aboard the Beaver Line's *Lake Superior,* due in Halifax in a fortnight's time.

The Doukhobors were ill-prepared for the forty-five below (-43° C) weather. They wore hard leather boots and pieces of blanket around their feet in place of socks. The women wore only a half slipper with a leather sole. Nobody had mitts. Several froze their toes. McCreary bought two hundred pairs of moccasins, four hundred pairs of socks, and a mountain of warm clothing for the men he was dispatching to prepare the new colonies for the others.

The staple food was simplified. Cheese, molasses, and fish, which some had been fed at Brandon and Portage La Prairie, were cut off because the Doukhobors themselves insisted they all get the same provisions. The regular diet would be potatoes, onions, cabbage, tea and sugar.

Meanwhile, McCreary had managed to outfit and

supply gangs of ten men from each of the three colonies planning to settle in the West. These were out cutting timber for houses. By February 9, one gang had erected three buildings in the settlement, each large enough to hold fifty or sixty people.

So, with their own resources, the Doukhobors rose to the challenge. The young men took any job they could get, from shovelling snow to chopping wood. The older men set up cottage industries, making wooden spoons and painted bowls for sale. The women responded to local demand for fine embroidery and woven woollens. The younger girls took jobs as domestic servants.

Rather than purchase shovels and harnesses, the Doukhobor farmers bought iron bars and leather, built forges to produce implements, and fashioned Russian-style gear that was superior to the mass-produced Canadian harness.

The Dominion Experimental Farm gave advice on crops. The Massey-Harris Company sold equipment on credit. And so, with the help of a number of dedicated and generous friends, these extraordinary people were on the way to self-sufficiency.

In spite of all the problems, Canada, in just over a year, managed to settle seventy-five hundred persecuted and poverty-stricken Russians on the black soil of Saskatchewan in three separate colonies. One, known as the Rosthern Colony, lay just west of that town on the South Saskatchewan River. The so-called North and South colonies lay to the southeast, the first on the Manitoba border, the other just north of Yorkton.

Within a year, their villages were built and their future seemed secure. But trouble was brewing in the North and South colonies. To a small and fanatical group, the true promised land wasn't in Saskatchewan at all, but in the dreams and visions of their leaders.

The Doukhobors believed that Christ lived in every man and so priests were unnecessary and the Bible obsolete. They rejected churches, litany, icons, and festivals. They insisted their only allegiance was to Christ – they would take no oaths to a government. They were fanatically loyal to their leader, Peter Verigin. He was still in exile in Siberia, but from Siberia he could send messages to the Canadian colonies.

The Doukhobors did not believe in the concept of private property, and because of this they were bound to come into open conflict with the Canadian government. The Doukhobors held their property in common, pooling their resources and farming big tracts of land. But the rigid Canadian system didn't allow that. Each quarter section was owned by an individual who had title to it. Each Canadian family lived on that quarter section – often miles from their nearest neighbours. The Doukhobors, however, lived close together in villages.

In that first summer there was scarcely an able-bodied man left in any of the fifty-seven villages. While they worked on the railway, the women broke the sod, often hitching themselves to ploughs – twenty-four to each team.

By the end of 1900, the men were back at work in the fields. Life was hard but there was also an idyllic quality to it. A choir chanted in the streets each morning to wake the workers. The men divided into gangs and sang as they marched towards the fields. The town meeting made for a rough democracy. Antelope and deer foraged unmolested among the cattle, for these people were vegetarians.

They were incredibly polite: they never passed each other on the street without removing their caps and bowing. It was explained that they were not really bowing to each other but to the spirit of Jesus within them.

The general attitude towards the Doukhobors in Canada was one of curiosity and good nature. After all, they were a persecuted people fleeing from a tyrannical government.

And then, in the fall of 1902, a stunning series of events occurred that would put the Spirit Wrestlers back on the front pages and from then on make the name Doukhobor a synonym for terror, fanaticism, and lunacy.

In all his years on the prairies, Wes Speers, the colonization agent, had never seen anything like it, and he knew he would never see anything like it again. It was October 27, 1902. He was standing on the open prairies, some thirteen miles (21 km) north of Yorkton – a tall, rangy figure, Sifton's appointee as colonization agent for the West – waiting for the Doukhobors.

They came upon him slowly like a black cloud, low on the prairie, densely packed, thirty to forty abreast – some two thousand men, women, and children. The procession was headed by an old man with a flowing white beard, chanting and waving his hands. Behind him, two stalwart Russians led a blind man, followed by men bearing stretchers of poplar branches and blankets carrying the sick, and behind them a choir, three hundred strong. The chanting never stopped, the multitude repeating the verses of the Twenty-second Psalm over and over again: "*My God, my God, why hast thou forsaken me?*"

For the next two weeks, Speers would come head to head with the most stubborn group of fanatics in Western Canada – the splinter group of Doukhobors who called themselves the Sons of God. These people seemed intent on killing themselves in the name of the Saviour, not by any sudden action but simply from hunger and exposure on the frostbitten prairie.

The government faced a dilemma: it could not allow them to die, neither could it interfere with a devout religious sect. There must be no violence: after all, they didn't intend to harm anybody but themselves.

Slowly, the army of men, women, and children advanced on the colonization agent. He knew it was useless to reason with them. They required nothing of him, they said.

"We are going to seek Christ," they told him vaguely. Christ, apparently, was somewhere in the southeast, somewhere in the land of the sun, far from the windswept prairie, in a country where the fruit hung thickly on the trees and vegetables were cropped the year round, where it was not necessary to use a single animal for labour, food, or clothing. A lovely prospect for people facing another bitter winter – but a false one.

The pale prairie afternoon would soon turn to dusk. Speers knew that he must find immediate shelter for these people who believed that God would look after them. Back he rode to Yorkton to arrange for space in the immigration hall, the Orange Hall, an implement warehouse, a pool hall, a grain elevator. Some of the children were crying with hunger. The people were living on dried rose-hips, herbs,

Almost 2,000 Sons of God Doukhobors march across the prairies in search of a promised land.

leaves, and grasses. The women of Yorkton were prepared to feed them – that is, if they agreed to be fed.

Speers had picked up the first rumours of trouble that summer when he heard that some of the Doukhobors in the Yorkton area were acting strangely. They were freeing all their animals, burning their sheepskin vests and leather boots, making sandals from plaited binder twine, refusing to eat eggs, butter, or milk, abandoning their horses and hitching themselves as teams, and making no provision for

the coming winter by putting up hay for their stock. Some had come to believe that it was a sin to exploit animals in any way.

The problem had its roots in the complex mind of Peter Verigin, resting comfortably in Siberian exile and day-dreaming of a paradise on earth in which the sun would always shine, where men would live on fruit and never exploit their animal brethren, where money would not be needed, and metal, the symbol of an industrial society, would be outlawed.

Verigin's vague ideas took hold. For more than fifteen years, members of the sect had been without anyone to guide them. They were hungry for leadership, especially by 1902, when the Canadian government began to press upon them demands they could not accept. Canada didn't want them to hold land in common. In addition, it wanted every Doukhobor to take an oath of allegiance to the state. Now, out of the blue, came a message from the one man who could stand up for them against the same kind of authority that had forced them to leave Russia.

There was more, surely. There must also have been a longing for the kind of sunny paradise that Verigin dreamed of, where frost never fell, winds did not blow, and prairie white-outs were unknown. The exiled leader had talked of warmth and energy from the sun: "Man employing food raised by an abundance of solar heat, such as, for instance, raspberries, strawberries... tender fruits, his organism will be formed, as it were, of energy itself...."

Slowly, a sect within a sect was forming – the Sons of God. Self-appointed apostles began moving through the villages, spreading the new gospel. And so there they were on the night of October 27 – men, women, and children huddled together in a poplar bluff without a fire to warm them.

Their leaders insisted that they would continue to go on to find Christ, but Speers had no intention of allowing that. With the help of the Mounted Police he herded the resisting women into shelter, guarded by three mounted policemen and fifteen constables. The men, he said, were free to continue if they wanted to. The following day, after standing up praying and chanting all night, they set off again.

They threw away the clothes they'd bought in Yorkton, leaving behind a trail of boots, cloaks, and hats. They slept in ditches, lived on grasses and raw potatoes until their faces grew gaunt and their eyes feverish. And yet they still managed to walk twenty miles (32 km) a day, their feet torn and bleeding from the frost-covered stubble. Speers trailed them trying to make them listen to reason, but the answer was always the same: "Jesus will look after us."

On November 7, 450 hard-core believers reached Minnedosa, in Manitoba. They intended to carry on, but Speers had no intention of letting them.

All night long the Sons of God, herded into the local skating rink, prayed and sang. The Doukhobors tried to rush the doors but were prevented. A special train was on its way with twenty-three police. It arrived at 4:30 that afternoon. Speers led the men out of the rink. The Douk-hobors turned from him and started to head east. The townspeople stopped them.

Several were picked up bodily and flung into the train because the Sons of God refused to strike a blow against their captors. It took forty minutes to pack them into the waiting cars and send them home.

That broke the back of the pilgrimage. The women and children had already been taken back to the railhead near their villages. They refused to ride the rest of the way and insisted on walking the full twenty-seven miles (43 km). Within two hours of their return, they had their furnaces going, vegetable soup on the stove, and were hard at work scrubbing and cleaning their houses.

For the Doukhobors the pilgrimage left a bitter legacy. It turned public opinion against them. The opposition press began to rail against all Doukhobors – whether or not they belonged to the minority sect. The urge to turn them into carbon copies of Canadians was just as strong as it was in the case of the Galicians.

Meanwhile the villages were at peace. Exhausted by their long travail, the Sons of God rested quietly, waiting for the imminent arrival of their leader, Peter Verigin, released at last from his Siberian confinement.

CHAPTER SEVEN

~

Peter the Lordly

VERIGIN ARRIVED IN WINNIPEG on a perfect winter afternoon just three days before Christmas, 1902. He started down the platform to a crowd of greeters – a big man, half a head taller than his fellow passengers, with a luxuriant black beard and dark thoughtful eyes. He was not dressed like the others. Under his short gabardine coat, one could see leggings, close-fitting, dark grey, piped with black. He wore a black fedora, and around his neck on a long cord dangled a silver watch and a gold pencil.

His supporters rushed toward him. He dropped his black nickel-studded valise, removed his hat, stretched out his arms to embrace the woman who led the greeters. "Anna!" he cried. She was his sister; they had not seen each other for fifteen years.

Both the Doukhobors and the Immigration Department saw Verigin as a saviour. The sect was convinced he would stand up for their rights. The government was hopeful he would calm the fanatics.

For the next three days, from early morning until late in

Peter the Lordly greets his followers.

the evening, Peter Vasilivich Verigin received representatives from each of the fifty-seven villages. They called him Peter the Lordly, and the title fitted. Off he went on a tour of all the villages, seated in a six-horse sleigh, with a choir of maidens chanting psalms. The authorities were delighted. They were convinced that Verigin would bring peace.

He was a good bargainer for his people – he got the railway contractors to raise the Doukhobors' wages. One contractor tried to tell him that if he went too high the company couldn't make a profit.

"No company will profit by our work," Verigin told him. "Take it or leave it." The contractor took it because workmen were hard to find.

Verigin swiftly changed from his Russian costume to a tailored suit with a white shirt and turned-down collar. He had his long hair close-cropped and his face clean-shaven except for a bristling moustache. He said he would give his children Canadian names.

The community was still split into three factions. The well-to-do farmers of the Rosthern Colony, southwest of Prince Albert, were opting more and more for independence and free enterprise. The radical Left, especially in the South Colony near Yorkton, were activists who believed in demonstrations to reach their goals. In the centre was the great mass of Doukhobors who wanted to retain the communal system of central villages where personal possessions were all but unknown. That too was Verigin's desire, but he became more and more unsure of achieving it in Saskatchewan.

He travelled about like an Oriental leader, in a six-horse sleigh in winter and in a carriage in summer, wearing a silk hat. The inevitable choir of chanting maidens accompanied him. One, a plump, blue-eyed brunette of eighteen, Anastasia Golubova, he called his wife.

But his power was dwindling. The first of a series of small protest marches engineered by the same fanatics who had led the pilgrimage of 1902 took place in the following March. Fifty of them refused to register their lands with the government. They began to travel from village to village urging their fellows to resist temptation, to turn animals loose, and to seek the sun.

Meanwhile a new group, the Freedomites, known as the "Sons of Freedom," added two new rituals – first nudity, later arson. The results for Verigin were catastrophic.

The press was intrigued by men, women, and children who burned their clothes and marched naked on the chill prairie. The authorities stopped all efforts to photograph them. Speers tried to find out why they would insist on taking off their clothes, and was told it was part of their religion – that they wanted to go to a warm country and live like Adam and Eve.

That did not endear them to the Canadian public. Some went to jail where, being vegetarians, they lived on raw potatoes and oatmeal. Others followed on charges of arson, and two were judged insane. One died of malnutrition, and the headlines kept on.

The Doukhobors had no political power. Because they refused to swear allegiance to Canada they couldn't become citizens and vote. Squatters moved onto their unregistered lands, and these had clout in Ottawa. With tens of thousands of settlers moving into the West, the Doukhobors' holdings looked good to them. Pressure began to mount, and then Sifton resigned and Frank Oliver replaced him as Minister of the Interior.

Oliver's intentions were to treat the Doukhobors like any other landowners. They must conform to Canadian customs. There would be no exceptions to the rigid regulations of the Homestead Act. Each must obey its regulations to build his house on his free quarter section and farm it individually.

Communal farming was out. There could be no villages as a result, no common tilling of the soils. The houses would be scattered about, four to a section, in the Canadian fashion. If any Doukhobor continued to live in the villages, his ownership would be cancelled. Only a few people protested this violent attempt at assimilation. Few Canadians seemed to care.

Verigin had seen it coming. He had no intention of submerging his people's religion and lifestyle in an ocean of Canadian conformity. The short haircut and the clean-shaven face had lulled the authorities into believing the Doukhobor leader was like everybody else. He was far more complicated, determined, and far-sighted than outward appearances suggested.

He'd built up a massive war chest by sending the men of

his flock to earn money on the railways. With these funds he decided to buy other lands privately in another province – in the Kootenay district of British Columbia – and start all over again. For the first and only time, a substantial body of immigrants rejected the Canadian dream and turned its back on the promised land.

This was an incredible sacrifice. Everything the Doukhobors had slaved for since 1899 was to be abandoned – the neatly ploughed fields, the well-kept villages, the stacks of hay, the lofts bursting with grain. Not everybody followed Verigin. Two thousand independent Doukhobors at Rosthern took the oath and settled on their individual homesteads. Another thousand in two colonies north of Yorkton decided also to remain. But five thousand followed their leaders to the new province.

Suddenly, in June, 1907, a quarter of a million acres (100,000 hectares) of prime farm land, abandoned by the Doukhobors, came onto the market – free homesteads for any man who could fight for a place in the long lineups forming at the doors of the land offices.

This wasn't raw land. Some of these homesteads were worth from three thousand to ten thousand dollars. And so the stage was set for the last great land rush in North America.

There were scenes of mob violence in Yorkton and Prince Albert. Over the weekend of June 1 and 2, men waited for forty-five hours in the cold and rain for the Yorkton office to open at nine on Monday morning. The town was crammed with real estate speculators. Hotels were bursting. People paid ten cents a night just to sleep in haystacks.

Far more people queued up each night than there were homesteads available. In Prince Albert, one group of thirty exhausted and shivering men, bone weary after more than twenty-four hours in line, found themselves muscled from their positions by a fresher party. They were crushed so tightly that some were shoved through the glass panes of the land office. Five policemen had to restore order with fists and clubs.

By the first week in June the police figured that five hundred strangers, representatives of real estate men, were in Yorkton with orders to break into the queue at any cost. During one night a group of these men charged the line and struggled with the Mounted Police. "Mob the police! Mob the police!" they cried, until the sergeant in charge called out the fire department and turned a hose on them. But, dripping wet, they clung stubbornly to their place in the queue.

Thus the reign of Peter the Lordly came to an end on the prairies, with fists and truncheons, cries and catcalls, and the jarring sounds of human beings in collision – a stark contrast to the soft chanting of the choir of maidens, now only an echo in the empty villages scattered along the green valleys of Saskatchewan.

Looking back, the government's new attitude, under Frank Oliver, towards the Doukhobors seems not only racist but foolhardy. Why shouldn't people work communally? Why do they have to be separated by long distances with a house on each quarter section – a lonely life for all immigrants who arrived in Canada? Why couldn't they cluster in villages?

Canada, in those days, was intent on bending all immigrants to its will – not only Galicians and Doukhobors, but also the English, the Americans, and the other nationalities who, a million strong, crowded into Canada in this restless, difficult, and eventually triumphant period.

In the end they managed to cling to their roots and their origins and their culture, while at the same time becoming strong Canadians. Many became important citizens – mayors of cities, leading politicians, lawyers and doctors, journalists and writers, engineers, and some just plain farmers. One, as we've already noted, became Governor General of Canada.

It was this vast horde of strangers filling up an empty land that eventually helped to build a country stretching from ocean to ocean. They helped give their adopted country its greatest natural resource – grain. They remain proud of their origins – and in this sense the government helped them by making Canada the first multicultural country in the world. But they also strengthened the land and were responsible for the great Western boom that helped make the country prosperous in the days before the First World War when Wilfrid Laurier said the twentieth century belonged to Canada.

INDEX

Coming Soon
A Prairie Nightmare

Isaac Montgomery Barr was a Christian minister with a vision of settling western Canada with industrious Anglo-Saxon farm families. But were his ambitions entirely honourable?

In 1903 Barr brought 2,000 unsuspecting British colonists to what is now Saskatchewan and eastern Alberta. "Agriculture is simple," he had told them before they embarked. "The work is not very hard." But hard it most certainly was …

In the third instalment of *Canada Moves West,* Pierre Berton presents a lively recreation of the life and times of Isaac Barr, the false promises he made, and the hard lives his followers endured.